This book belongs to:

Sew much fabric. Sew little time!

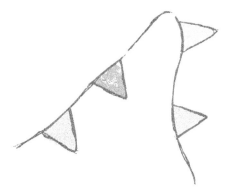

Beautiful things come together one stitch at a time

When life gives you scraps, make a quilt!

Eat. Sleep. Sew. Repeat.

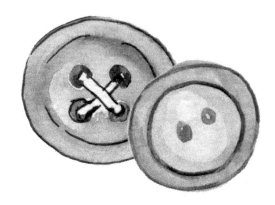

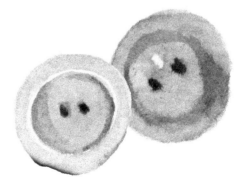

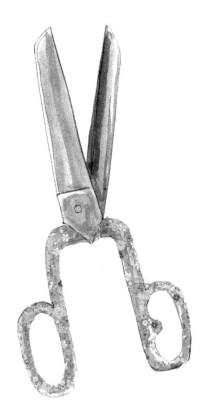

Sewing makes everything better!

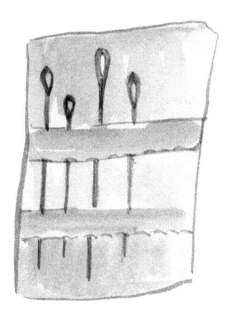

Relieving stress one stitch at a time!

Keep Calm and Sew On

May your bobbin always be full

Sewing is a work of heart

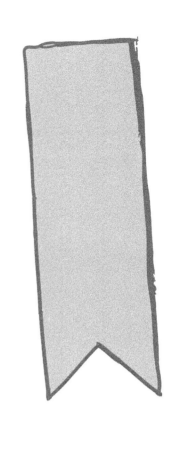

Life is sew beautiful

Behind every sewer is a huge stash of fabric!

Sewing warms the heart and feeds the soul!

I sew because it's cheaper than therapy!

Sew crafty!

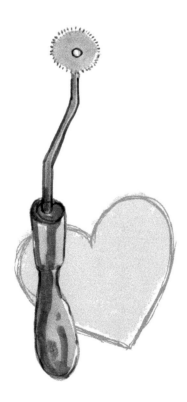

Never underestimate the power of a woman with a sewing machine!

Happiness is a full bobbin!

Measure twice. Cut once!

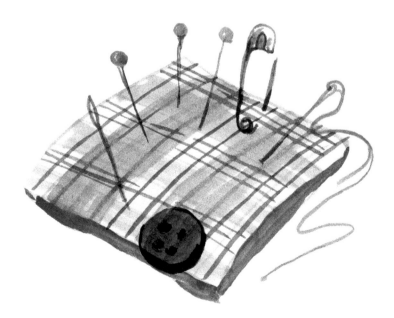

My soul is fed with needle and thread!

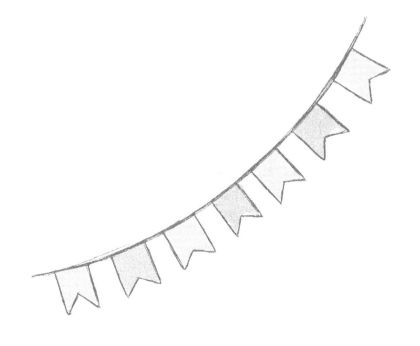

A good day is a day spent sewing

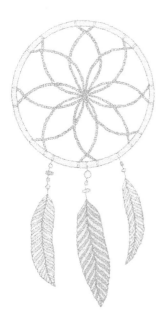

Don't dream it. Sew it!

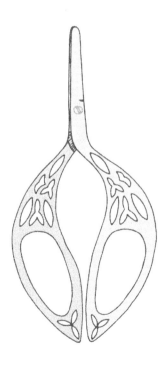

She who dies with the most fabric wins!

What I make with my hands, I give of my heart

To sew or not to sew? Duh!

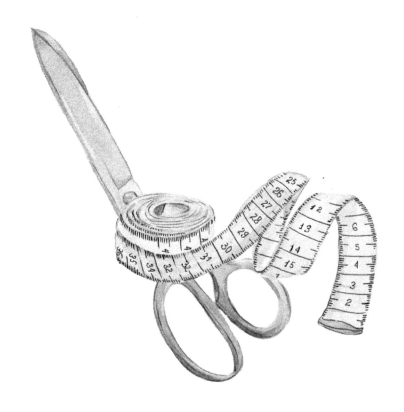

If sewing is not the answer, you asked the wrong question

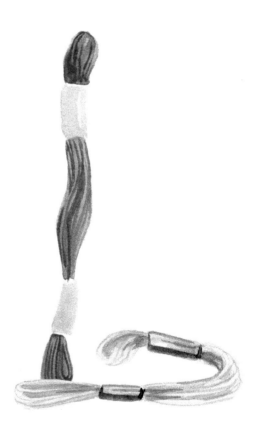

Sewing Forever. Housework whenever!

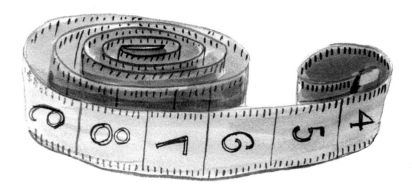

Friends are like fabric. You can never have enough!

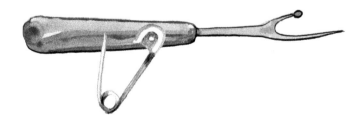

A yard a day keeps the blues away!

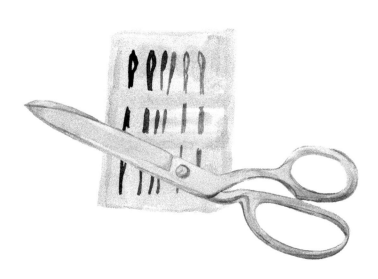

I like to party. And by party I mean stay home and sew!

A clean house is a sign of a broken sewing machine!

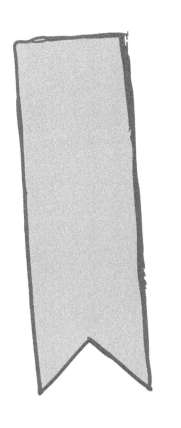

I don't want to look back and think
"I should have bought that fabric!"

CPSIA information can be obtained
at www.ICGtesting.com
Printed in the USA
LVHW021021201218
601201LV00004B/640/P